TAKE heart!

COMPANION JOURNAL
BY MARY BETH WOLL, MA, LMHC & LINDA SMITH, BS

All Scriptures are quoted from the New International Version.

©2024 The Widows Project

All rights reserved. No portion of this book may be reproduced, stored in a retrieval system, or transmitted in any form or by any means—electronic, mechanical, photocopy, recording, scanning or other—except for brief quotations in critical reviews or articles, without the prior written permission of the authors.

ISBN paperback: **978-1-7362169-8-9**

David Woll: Cover Design
Kristi Knowles: Interior Layout/Design

Take Heart Journal Introduction

Take Heart! has a very definite purpose and goal—to offer you healing support during your grieving process. We want to help you recover from your devastating loss so you can move forward into a life of effectiveness for God, becoming fruitful; even 30, 60, and 100 times more productive than you ever were before (Mark 4:20).

We have designed this journal to be used as a companion to Take Heart! A Widowed Man's Guide to Growing Stronger. Each chapter has a Growing Stronger Guideline with an accompanying life principle and Scripture.

How to use this journal:

Each week, as you prepare for and meet with your Take Heart! group, we have provided space in your journal for:

1. Study notes,
2. Meeting notes, and
3. Reflections.

The authors of Take Heart!, Bruce McLeod and Rev. Chris Taylor, and the authors of this journal care about you! We have been where you are now. We pray that God will bless you with His love and comfort as you grow stronger in your Take Heart! journey.

With love and prayers,

Mary Beth and *Linda*

Mary Beth Woll, MA, LMHC
Linda Smith, BS

Growing Stronger Guideline #1

Keep first things first

Develop an intimate relationship with Jesus
because you are powerless to overcome grief
in your own strength.

*"The Lord is close to the brokenhearted and saves those
who are crushed in spirit" (Psalm 34:18).*

Study Notes

Meeting Notes

Further Reflection

GROWING STRONGER GUIDELINE #2:

BALANCE SUFFERING IN COMMUNION AND COMMUNITY

Give your Broken Heart to God and His People
to Receive healing from both.

*"The Spirit of the Sovereign Lord is on me...
He has sent me to bind up the brokenhearted"
(Isaiah 61:1).*

Study Notes

Meeting Notes

Further Reflection

GROWING STRONGER GUIDELINE #3:
CONNECTION LEADS TO FREEDOM

To become truly healed, share your story with safe, significant others as well as with Jesus.

"The Spirit of the Sovereign Lord is on me ... to proclaim freedom for the captives and release from darkness for the prisoners" (Isaiah 61:1).

Study Notes

Meeting Notes

Further Reflection

GROWING STRONGER GUIDELINE #4:
THROW OFF WHAT HINDERS

With God's help, get rid of It!

"Therefore, since we are surrounded by such a great cloud of witnesses, let us throw off everything that hinders and the sin that so easily entangles, and let us run with perseverance the race marked out for us" (Hebrews 12:1).

Study Notes

Meeting Notes

Further Reflection

GROWING STRONGER GUIDELINE #5:

KEEP LOOKING UP

Make *Personal Growth* an even higher priority
than resolving your grief.

*"And the peace of God, which transcends all understanding,
will guard your hearts and your minds in Christ Jesus"
(Philippians 4:7).*

Study Notes

Meeting Notes

Further Reflection

Growing Stronger Guideline #6:

Stand Strong

Whenever you feel like giving up, endure.

"Be alert and of sober mind. Your enemy the devil prowls around like a roaring lion, looking for someone to devour"
(I Peter 5:8).

Study Notes

Meeting Notes

Further Reflection

GROWING STRONGER GUIDELINE #7:

TAKE HEART!

When you experience correction, remind yourself that God is a good Father and say, "My Abba (Daddy) Father loves me."

"No discipline is enjoyable while it is happening—it's painful! But afterward, there will be a peaceful harvest of right living for those who are trained in this way" (Hebrews 12:11).

Study Notes

Meeting Notes

Further Reflection

Growing Stronger Guideline #8:

Run Your Race

Remember, your victory is just around the corner.

"Therefore, since we are surrounded by such a great cloud of witnesses, let us throw off everything that hinders and the sin that so easily entangles, and let us run with perseverance the race marked out for us" (Hebrew 12:1).

"Therefore, strengthen your feeble arms and weak knees. Make level paths for your feet, so that the lame may not be disabled, but rather healed" (Hebrews 12:12–13).

Study Notes

Meeting Notes

Further Reflection

GROWING STRONGER GUIDELINE #9:

REMEMBER, GOD IS ON YOUR SIDE

God's love is based on His Love for you, not your performance.

*"Even to your old age and gray hairs I am He,
I am He Who will sustain you.
I have made you and I will carry you; I will sustain
you and I will rescue you" (Isaiah 46:4).*

Study Notes

Meeting Notes

Further Reflection

Growing Stronger Guideline #10:
Grieve With Company

Weep with those who weep until God,
Himself, wipes away all your tears.

"The Spirit of the Lord is on me...to comfort all who mourn, and provide for those who grieve in Zion—to bestow on them a crown of beauty instead of ashes, the oil of gladness instead of mourning, and a garment of praise instead of a spirit of despair" (Isaiah 61:2b–3).

Study Notes

Meeting Notes

Further Reflection

Growing Stronger Guideline #11:

Let Your Light Shine

Grow stronger through your loss
and become a blessing to others.

*"They will be called oaks of righteousness,
a planting of the LORD for the display of His splendor.
They will rebuild the ancient ruins and restore the places long
devastated; they will renew the ruined cities that have been
devastated for generations" (Isaiah 61:3-4).*

Study Notes

Meeting Notes

Further Reflection

Growing Stronger Guideline #12:

Leave a Legacy

When you glorify God through your grief, you become an example that will encourage generations to come.

"They will rebuild the ancient ruins and restore the places long devastated; they will renew the ruined cities that have been devastated for generations" (Isaiah 61:4).

Study Notes

Meeting Notes

Further Reflection